WAC SNAX

ARABELLA WARNER
with
TOMMY BOYD and JAMES BAKER

ILLUSTRATED BY TONY
BLUNDELL

CORGI BOOKS

Also published by Corgi Books

WAC JOKES
WAC GHOSTS, MONSTERS AND
LEGENDS
WAC ONE-MINUTE MYSTERIES

WIDE AWAKE CLUB: WAC SNAXS
A CORGI BOOK 0 552 542814

First published in Great Britain by Corgi
Books

PRINTING HISTORY
Corgi edition published 1986

Corgi Books are published by Transworld Publishers Ltd., 61-63 Uxbridge
Road, Ealing, London W5 5SA.

Printed and bound in Great Britain by
Cox & Wyman Ltd, Reading

CONTENTS

FOREWORD

To all WACsnackers,

All the recipes in this book can be made in a matter of minutes. So if you're forgotten your Mum's birthday, you've feeling a bit peckish during a WAC commercial break, or you've left five minutes to make your packed lunch before the school bus goes – don't despair. Use this book to get you out of a pickle.

Of course, when you're racing against time, things don't always turn out according to plan. But whatever happens, don't throw a wobbly. Calmness in the kitchen is the number one rule. We can't always be perfect – remember James's marzipan bees, Los Trios Ringbarcus's crispy bars and Tommy, James and my untossable pancakes!

However short your deadlines, you must stick to club rules. Beware of sharp knives – we don't want any of your fingers ending up alongside the marmite ones. Make sure you get a helping hand from an adult if you're using the cooker – and if you've just changed the chain on your bike, it might be a good idea to wash your hands: lubricating oil doesn't tend to be a very good flavouring. And do clear up afterwards – we don't want the book banned from the house.

Above all, thanks to all wide-awakers who sent in recipes. We've had a really messy time making them up – we're only sorry we couldn't include them all.

Wacky snacking!

Arabella

Culinary Creatures

MOUTHWATERING MICE

What you need
1 Swiss roll
Butter icing (mix together 125g butter
and 250g icing sugar)
Almond flakes
Liquorice laces
Silver balls

What to do
Cut a slice from the Swiss roll for the
base of the body. Then mould the butter

icing over the cake into the shape of a mouse. Put two almond flakes in for ears, a liquorice lace for the tail and the silver balls for the eyes and nose.

How James did it
After you've finished moulding the mice, wash your hands – James ended up with silver balls, liquorice and almond flakes sticking all over him and none on the mice at all!

BABYBIRD CAKE

Ingredients
5 tablespoons icing sugar
Raspberry juice
1 chocolate sponge cake
Brown Smarties
2 glacé cherries

What to do
This is so easy even James can't make a mess of it. Put the icing sugar into a bowl, then add the raspberry juice – not

too much or it'll run all over the place. Spread it on top of the cake . . . then place the brown Smarties symmetrically on both sides of the cake and add two cherries for eyes. Simple, eh?

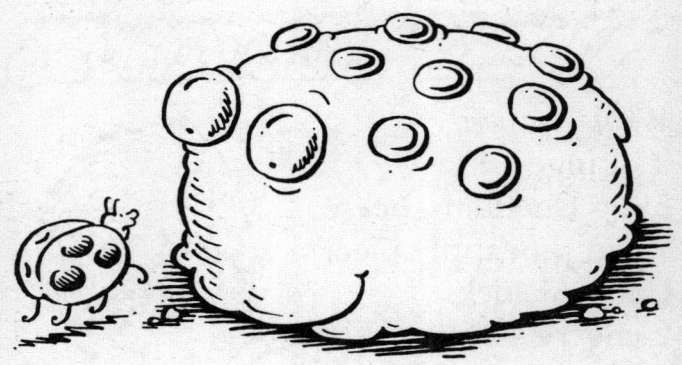

A slight variation for this is Measle Cake. Substitute water for the raspberry juice and red Smarties for the brown ones. It's a great medicine for someone sitting in bed with great big red spots.

From Emma Hobson,
North Humberside

WACKY HEDGEHOGS

What you need
2 oranges
500g Cheddar cheese
1 can pineapple pieces
Cocktail sticks
2 cherries

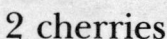

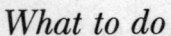

What to do
Cut a small slice from one end of each orange – you don't want your hedgehogs rolling all over the place. Then cut the

cheese into 1 cm cubes, and spear a piece of pineapple and a piece of cheese on to each cocktail stick. Push them in all over the oranges. For the eyes, cut the cherries in half, spear each half with a cocktail stick and stick them into the front of the oranges.

Try using different coloured cheese and fruit for different coloured hedgehogs.

From Teri-Anne Crates,
Lancashire

Arabella's alternative

Another way of making Wacky Hedgehogs is to use some leftover mashed potato, tomato ketchup, pre-cooked sausages and pickled onions. Mould the potato into a ball, cover in tomato ketchup, then stick the sausages in all over for spikes. Use the pickled onions for eyes . . . really makes your eyes water – yummy!

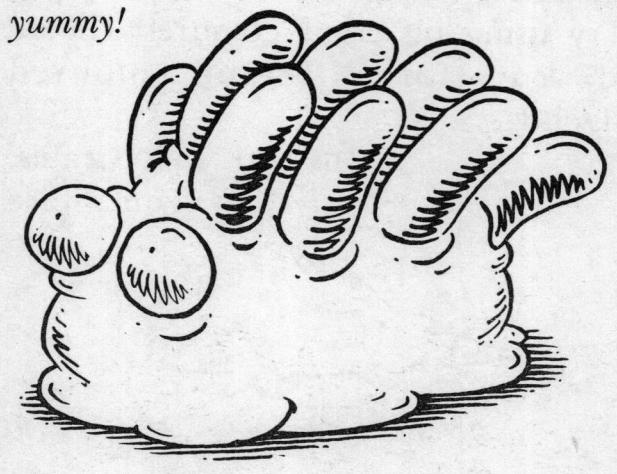

Gastronomic Games

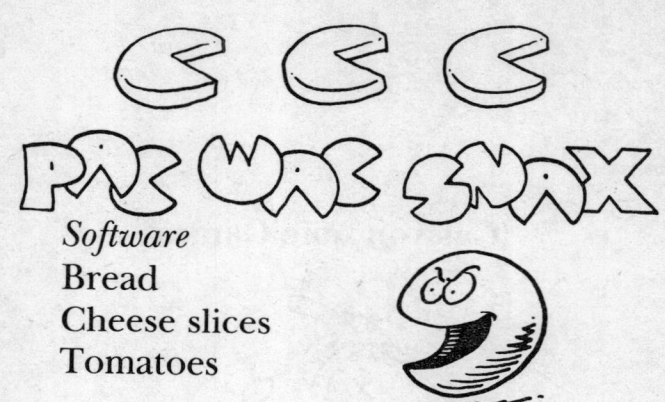

PAC WAC SNAX

Software
Bread
Cheese slices
Tomatoes

Programming
Take a slice of bread and toast it on one side. Put a piece of cheese on the

untoasted side. Cut the tomatoes into

slices, then cut a small triangle out of each slice. Put the Pacmen on to the cheese and grill until the cheese has melted.

Munch them before they munch you!

From Marc Short,
Liverpool

GOLF BALLS

Caddie's collection
14 digestive biscuits
1 small tin condensed milk
2 dessertspoons drinking chocolate
75g margarine (melted)
12 marshmallows
Desiccated coconut

Tactics
Don't just bash the biscuits loose on the table, or you'll find they all end up on the floor. Put them in a plastic bag, and then bash them into crumbs. Transfer

the crumbs into a mixing bowl and then add the condensed milk and drinking

chocolate. Stir in the melted margarine
to bind the mixture. Roll the marshmal-

lows in the mixture and then in the
desiccated coconut. Try catching them
in your mouth – you could get a hole in
one!

From Carole Rodgers,
  Co. Tyrone,
  Northern Ireland

CHEESE DOMINOES

Contents
25g butter
50g grated Cheddar cheese
Salt and pepper
Brown bread
Currants

How to play
Mix together butter, cheese and salt and

pepper. Cut the bread into rectangles.

Spread one side with the cheese mixture. Add the currants to form numbers on

the dominoes. Try getting through a game without eating them all!

From Kim Taylor,
Staffordshire

Jaw-jammers

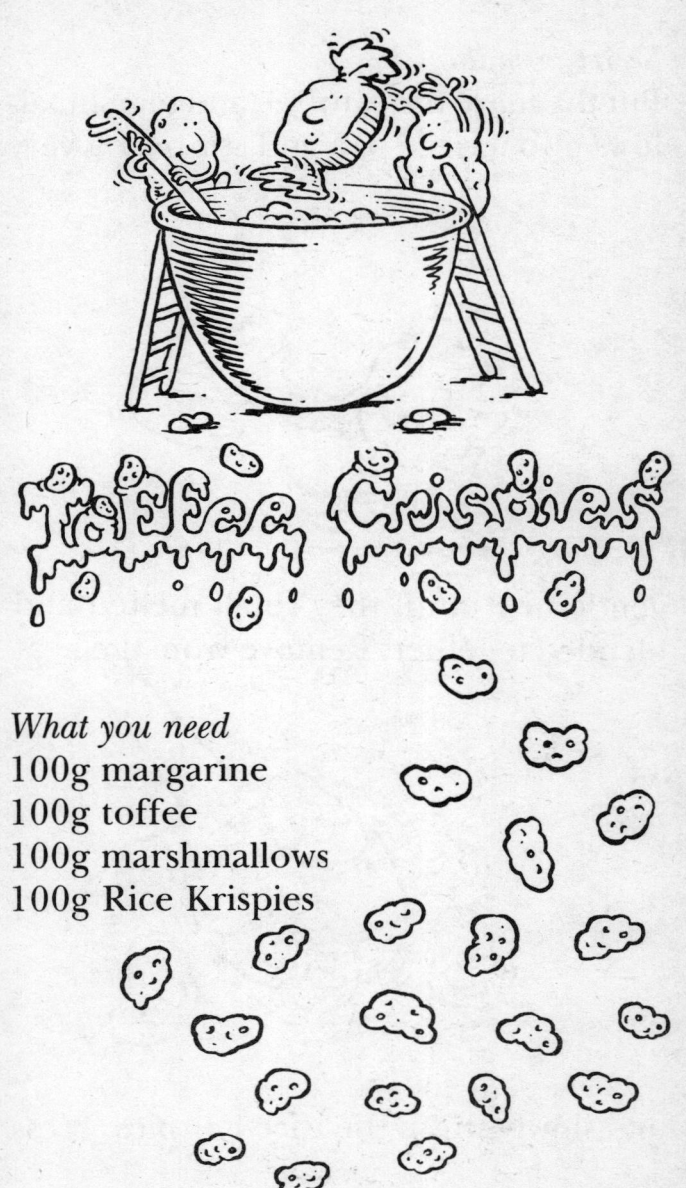

Toffee Crispies

What you need
100g margarine
100g toffee
100g marshmallows
100g Rice Krispies

Secret formula

Put the margarine, toffee and marshmallows into a large pan and stir over a very

gentle heat until they've all melted and
blended together. Remove from the heat

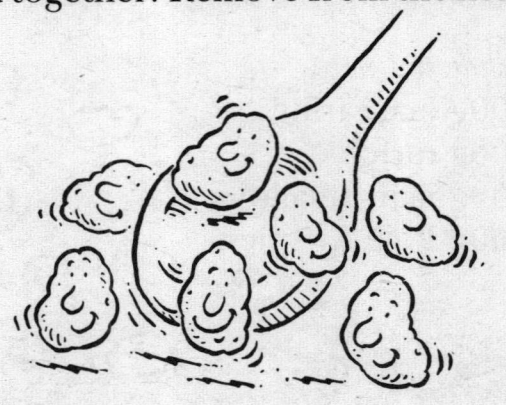

and slowly stir in the Rice Krispies. Press

the mixture into a greased tin and leave to cool.

Get your teeth stuck into that – and be careful of fillings!

From Mark Broadhurst,
Hungerford

(Crazy Paving)

What you need
100g butter
5 tablespoons golden syrup
100g icing sugar
3 tablespoons cocoa powder
Rind of 1 orange
$\frac{1}{2}$ packet Rich Tea biscuits

What to do
Melt the butter and golden syrup. Add the icing sugar, cocoa powder and orange rind, then fold in the crushed

Rich Tea biscuits (see Golf Balls, p18) and leave the mixture to cool. It does look a bit like crazy paving!

This was our very first WAC snack. I made it with David Bellamy, who stood on the kitchen table to pour in the treacle, which he did from a great height. Apparently he used to do it as a child, but it's not something I would recommend!

CHOCOLATE CRUNCH

What you need
100g butter
2 Mars Bars
100g Rice Krispies
12 squares cooking chocolate

What you do
Melt the butter first in a saucepan and then the Mars Bars. Add the Rice Kris-

pies and pour into a flat greased tin.

Melt the chocolate in a bowl over steaming hot water and then spread it over the Rice Krispie crunch. Leave it to cool.

A delicious jaw-jammer!

From Donna Lee,
Cleveland

Crunchy Creepy-crawlies

CENTIPEDE TOAST

What you need

1 stick French bread
Cheese
Ham
Cocktail sausages
Toothpicks
Pickled onions

What to do

This makes a great party piece. Cut the French bread in half and put the cheese

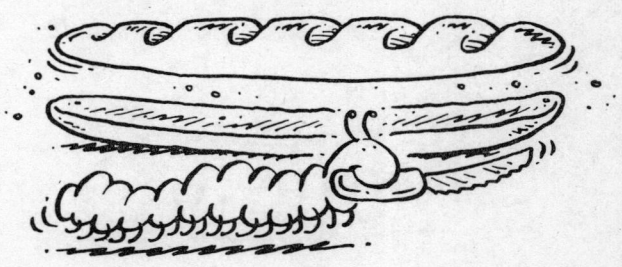

33

and ham in as filling. Stick the toothpicks in all around the edge for legs and then press the sausages on to the toothpicks.

The pickled onions can be used as eyes, pinned on to the front with two more toothpicks.

It makes a very scary centipede sandwich. You can use it to frighten your brother if he's been annoying you!

From Daphne Penna,
Oxford

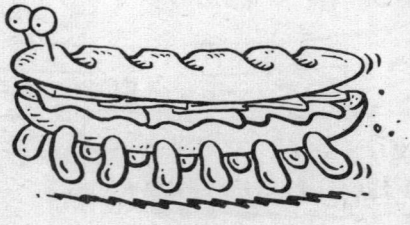

BUMBLE BEES

What you need
100g ground almonds
200g icing sugar
1 teaspoon almond essence
1 egg, beaten
1 tablespoon cocoa
1 packet chocolate buttons
Currants

What you do
Put the ground almonds into a bowl and sift in the icing sugar. Then add the

almond essence and the beaten egg. When the mixture becomes stiff, divide

35

it into balls. Flatten one side of the balls to make them stand on end, and brush

the top with cocoa powder – scrape a fork across to make stripes. Push two chocolate buttons into each bee for wings, and two currants for eyes. Try these for pudding after the centipede toast – but be careful, they can sting!

From Gretchen Marshall,
Bushey Heath, Hertfordshire

COLIN THE CATERPILLER

What you need
2 Swiss rolls (1 chocolate and 1 jam)
2 cocktail sticks
Glacé cherries

What you do
Colin the caterpillar can be put together in under a minute – I've timed it. It's a

great idea for your brother or sister's birthday – and it's very cheap to make.

Cut both Swiss rolls into 4cm slices. Alternate slices of chocolate Swiss roll with slices of jam Swiss roll, so that you end up with Colin's striped body. Stick

two cherries on to one end (with two cocktail sticks) for eyes. For feet, cut the remaining cherries in half and then into

slices and place at intervals under each side of the caterpillar's body. Then eat him quick before he crawls away!

From Deviner Gill,
Huntsworth, Birmingham

Flavourable Faces

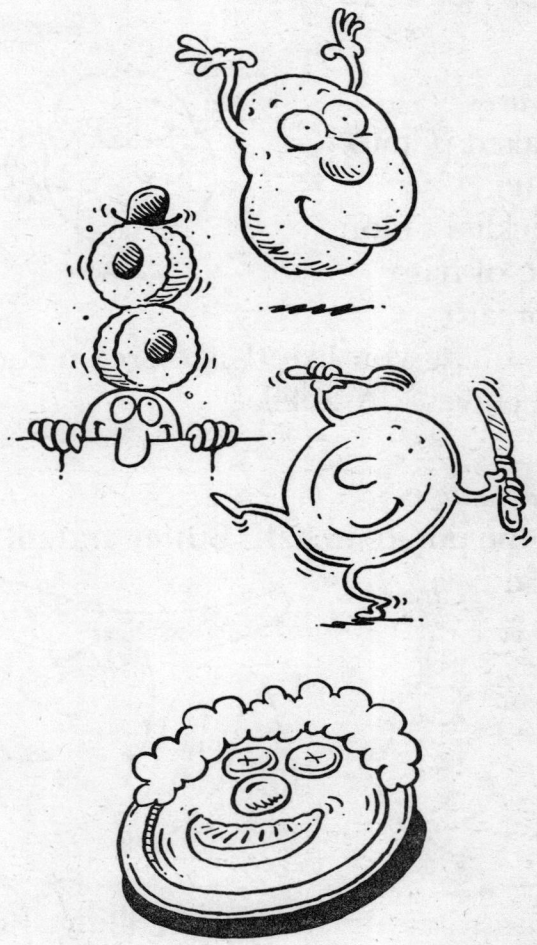

POTATO FACE

Features
1 baked potato
Butter
1 pickled onion
Slice of ham
1 tomato
Any filling you like (I like cream cheese and chives – Arabella!)

What to do
Cut the potato in half. Butter and fill the

potato with your choice of filling. Put a piece of ham in the middle so that it sticks out for the tongue, two slices of

the tomato for the eyes, then add the pickled onion for the nose. Try and

shape all the different features so they look like your friends!

From Mark Suddes,
Newton Hall, Durham

SWISS CHAD

What you need
1 Swiss roll
1 banana
2 round liquorice allsorts
Whipped cream (optional)

What to do
Cut half the Swiss roll into slices and stack them on top of each other to build a wall. You can cement them together

with whipped cream, though this is not essential. Use the other half of the Swiss roll as your Chad – stand it on end

behind the wall so that it appears to look over it. Place half the banana in the

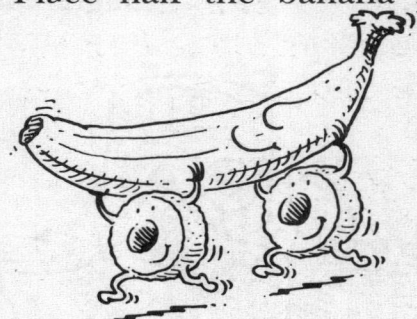

middle for a nose, and the liquorice

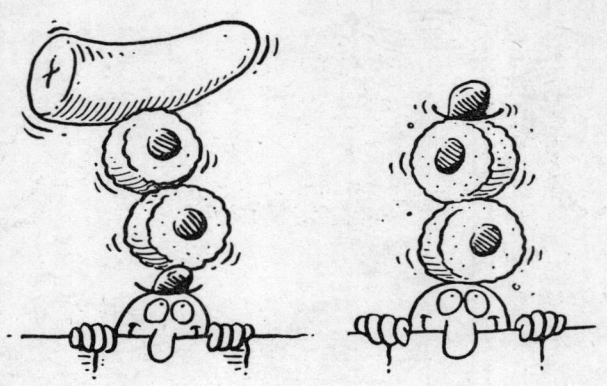

allsorts on either side for eyes. A nosey parker, Swiss Chad wide-awaker!

From Tony Robinson,
Dagenham, Essex

Face features
Mashed potato
2 beefburgers
2 fried eggs
1 tomato
Slice of toast
1 tin spaghetti

What to do
Get an adult to help you cook all the face features – they all have to be piping hot to make them taste nice. Spread the mashed potato evenly over a plate, then

place the two beefburgers on top as eyes. Trim off the edges of the fried eggs and put them on top of the beefburgers as pupils. Cut the tomato in half and use it as a nose, and use the leftover egg white to arrange into a mouth. Cut the toast into two triangles for a bow tie, and then

arrange the spaghetti around the head for hair. He's definitely based on Charles Golding – start eating from the bow tie upwards!

From Tori Downs,
Burnham-on-Couch, Essex

Features
1 fruit jelly
1 banana
1 grape
1 tangerine or orange
Whipped cream

How to do it

This is the sweet version of Mr Plate Face
– and very good for you! Dissolve the
fruit jelly in boiling water, pour into a

48

round bowl, and put it into the fridge to set. Cut two slices of banana for eyes, use

the grape for a nose and a segment of the orange for a mouth. Put the whipped cream at the top for hair. Try using the other bits of fruit for freckles, glasses and ribbons.

From Claire Bell,
Harshome Estate, Lincoln

Bed Bites

Bedclothes
2 slices of bread
Butter
Lettuce
Cucumber
Ham

Making it up
Spread two pieces of bread with butter, and then cut off the top of one piece – this shorter slice is the blanket. Cut the lettuce into strips and place on the whole

slice of bread – these are the sheets. You can just see the sleepers' heads above the

sheets – these are slices of cucumber. And, to make it a bit more colourful, there's an extra blanket – a piece of ham laid over the lettuce. Put the other blanket back on top, and then cut the

sandwich in half from top to bottom. Now you have two sleeping sandwiches – but make sure you set the alarm for Saturday morning. We wouldn't want your sandwiches to sleep through the Wide Awake Club!

From Ornella Galluccio,
Fulham, London

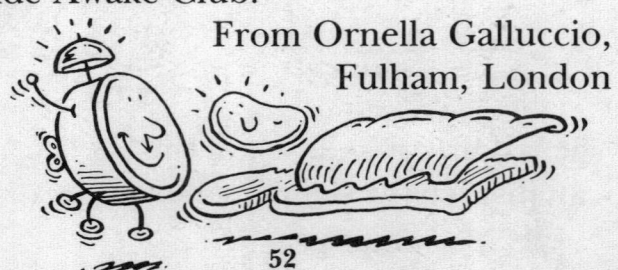

BABIES IN THEIR BEDS

You will need
Icing sugar
Chocolate buttons
Oblong-shaped biscuits
Jelly babies

What to do
Mix a small amount of icing sugar with a few drops of water to make a stiff paste.

Use this paste to stick a chocolate button upright at each end of the biscuits to look like headboards. These are the

beds. Then 'glue' a jelly baby (using the sugar paste) to the top, and that's it.

My Mum taught me this recipe when I was six, and I still make it for parties and packed lunches. You can make it easily in a minute. My record is five in 45 seconds, but it only takes a couple of seconds to eat them all!

FRIED EGG IN BED

What you need
1 slice of bread
1 egg
Oil

What to do
Cut quite a big hole in the middle of a slice of bread. Fry one side of the bread

in the oil – turn the bread over, and then break the egg carefully into the hole in

the middle of the bread. Fry until done. A perfect early morning WAC snack!

From Miss C. Ferguson,
Sydenham, London

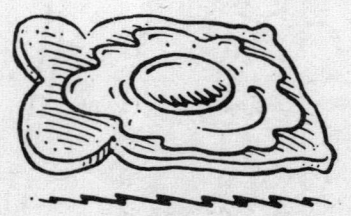

Snax for Pacs

"TRAFFIC" LIGHT SANDWICHES

What you need
2 slices of bread
Strawberry jam
Apricot jam
Greengage jam

What to do
Cut three round holes in a row from top to bottom in one slice of bread. Spread

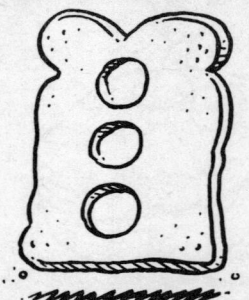

the top third of the other slice with

strawberry jam, the middle third with apricot jam, and the bottom third with greengage jam. Put the holey slice on

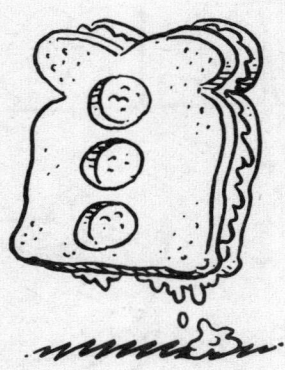

top, and you have your traffic-light sandwich. Start eating at the green light, but don't stop when you get to red!

From Sarah Williams,
Warley Werr, Midlands

DEVIL ROLLS

What you need
1 bread roll
Carrots
Butter
Grated cheese
Cucumber
Tomatoes

What to do
Cut the roll in half. Peel the carrots and cut off the ends – then place them at the top of the roll for horns. Butter the roll and cover in grated cheese. Use two

pieces of cucumber for eyes and a segment of the tomato for the mouth.

They should bring the devil out in you!
From Kay Wilson,
Roslin, Midlothian

CHOCOLATE HAYSTACK

What you need
Shredded wheat
1 large tin condensed milk
$\frac{1}{2}$ tin cocoa

What to do
Crush up enough shredded wheat with the condensed milk and cocoa to make a mushy mix in the bowl. Dip an egg into

cold water, and fill the dampened cup with some of the mixture. Turn it over

on to a plate and put it into the fridge to cool. Try sticking your pitchfork into that!

From Dawn Louise Owen,
Gosport, Hampshire

Munchy Monsters

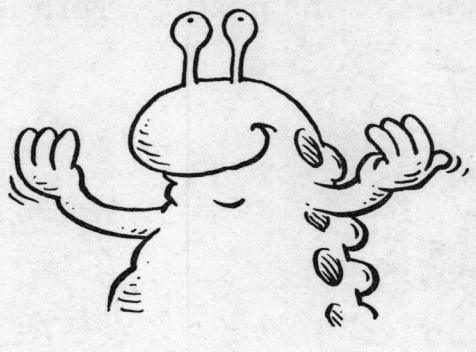

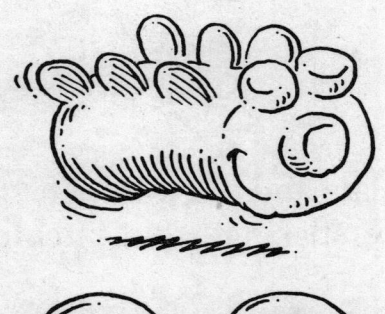

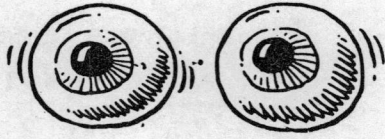

YUMMY MONSTERS

For 1 Monster Munch you will need

1 banana
Chocolate buttons
Hundreds and thousands
6 cocktail sticks
2 glacé cherries

What to do

Peel the banana and then stick the chocolate buttons in along its back like

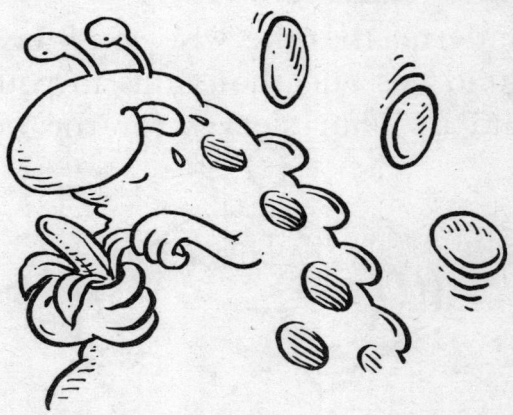

the spikes on a prehistoric monster.

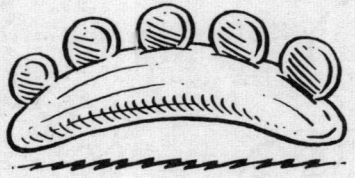

Sprinkle hundreds and thousands over the top – and do put a kitchen towel

underneath, otherwise you'll be finding hundreds and thousands in your shoes and up your sleeves for the next two

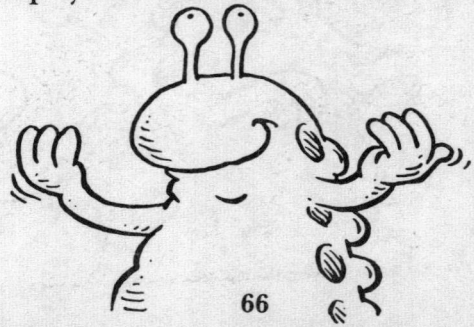

weeks! Take two of the cocktail sticks: one end goes into the cherries and the other into the top of the banana, so they look like eyes on stalks. Then take the

remaining four cocktail sticks and place them underneath as two pairs of legs.

Now munch the monster – if you dare!

From Paul Doucson,
Bracon Ash, Norfolk

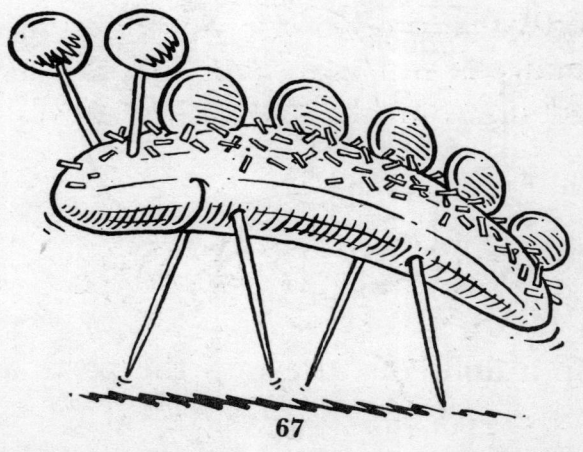

DOLLY MONSTERS

What you need
Scoop of soft margarine
1 teaspoon cocoa
Dolly mixtures
Chocolate mini rolls
Chocolate buttons
What to do
Mix the margarine and cocoa to a paste.

Dip a dolly mixture into the paste and

stick it on the end of the mini roll for a
nose. Do the same for the eyes. Break the

chocolate buttons in half and then, using
the paste for glue, stick these to the back
of the monster for spines.

From Alison Cole,
Selby, North Yorkshire

EYEBALLS

Contents
200g plain chocolate
150g butter
3 egg yolks
3 tablespoons sugar
3 teaspoons orange rind
3 tablespoons chocolate vermicelli

What to do
Soften the chocolate and butter in a small bowl over a pan of boiling water.

In a separate bowl heat the egg yolks and

sugar together. Add the chocolate and butter and then the orange rind. Put it in

the fridge until it begins to solidify but is not set hard. When it is a nice squidgy mixture, mould into balls – when you are doing this it's a good idea to moisten your hands with cold water, otherwise it

all sticks together. Then roll them in the
vermicelli to make them look like blood-

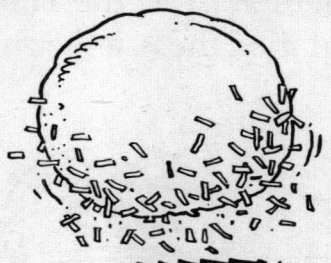

shot eyeballs. Try leaving them on a plate
full of raspberry juice to really frighten
your enemies.

From Helen Stanley,
Torquay, Devon

Sweet Treats

BEFORE 4 MINTS

What you need
100g plain chocolate
5 tablespoons icing sugar
1 tablespoon water
½ teaspoon peppermint
  essence

What to do
For everyone who goes to bed before eight o'clock, these are Before Four Mints. Break up half the chocolate and

melt it in a basin over a pan of boiling water. Pour the mixture on to a piece of greaseproof paper and spread it out

thinly. For the minty middle, mix together the icing sugar, water and peppermint essence. Beat until stiff and then spread evenly over the chocolate.

Melt the rest of the chocolate and pour over the peppermint icing. When it's set, cut it into squares.

Try making your own envelopes for them, and draw the WAC logo on the front.

From Helen James,
Enfield, Middlesex

TOMMY'S TICKLY TRUFFLE

What you need
50g cooking chocolate
25g margarine
$1\frac{1}{2}$ tablespoons icing sugar
1 egg yolk
$\frac{1}{2}$ teaspoon vanilla essence
1 tablespoon desiccated coconut

How to tickle Tommy's tummy
Break the chocolate into a bowl and melt
by placing over a pan of boiling water. In

a separate bowl, cream together the margarine and icing sugar – then add the

egg yolk and vanilla essence, stirring all the time. Slowly add the chocolate (if you pour it in too quickly it ends up looking

like curdled milk) and then leave it to thicken. Roll it into balls, coat them in coconut, and put into paper cases. How

simple can you get? No truffle at all!
From Stephanie Saunders,
Stamford, Lincolnshire

What you need
400g icing sugar
1 teaspoon glycerine
2 egg whites
½ teaspoon peppermint essence

What to do
These are called 'Safe Sweets' because there is no cooking involved – you'd need to be really accident prone to go wrong with them.

First, sift the icing sugar into a bowl – and then add the glycerine. Beat the egg

whites, and add a little at a time to the icing sugar to make a firm paste. Add the peppermint essence and then knead

until soft on a board sprinkled with icing sugar. Roll out the mixture 1 cm thick

and then cut out shapes using small shaped cutters. Place on a baking tray,

dust with icing sugar and leave to harden. And while you're making them, try saying this tongue-twister: 'She sells sixty-six safe sweets'!

From Corrall Davey,
Hemel Hempstead, Hertfordshire

Delicious Days

(for Shrove Tuesday)

What you need
250g flour
1 egg
½ pint milk
Butter

What to do
Jean Boxer sent us in this recipe for 'Don't Panic Pancakes' after she saw Tommy, James and me making such a

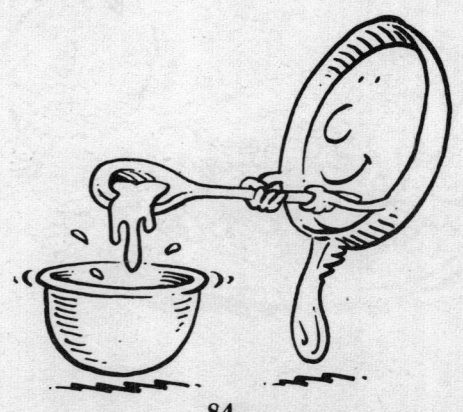

mess of ours. She says, mix the ingredients together until the consistency drips off the spoon. It mustn't be either too runny or too solid. Melt one teaspoon of butter in a frying pan and pour in four tablespoons of the batter. Don't attempt

to toss the pancakes until bubbles have formed – this tells you the underside is cooked. Then loosen the pancake and, apparently, the secret to perfect 'tossing'

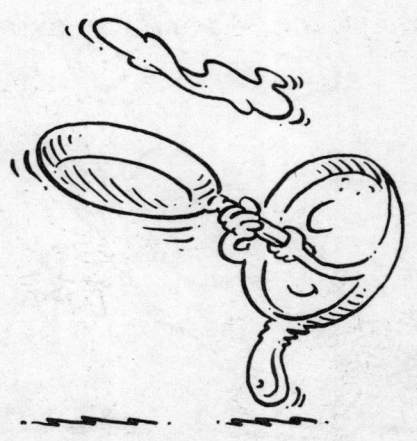

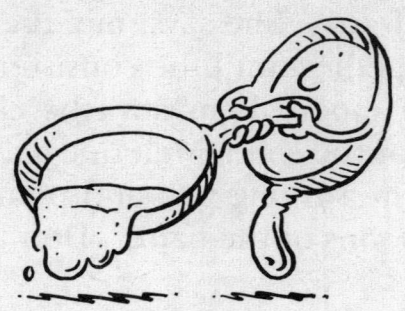

is to tilt the pan away from you, gently shaking the pancake to the edge and, just before it falls out, flip it up and over quickly – catching it, of course! She suggests honey, lemon and sugar, ice-cream, and peanut butter (yuk!) as fillings.

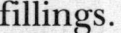

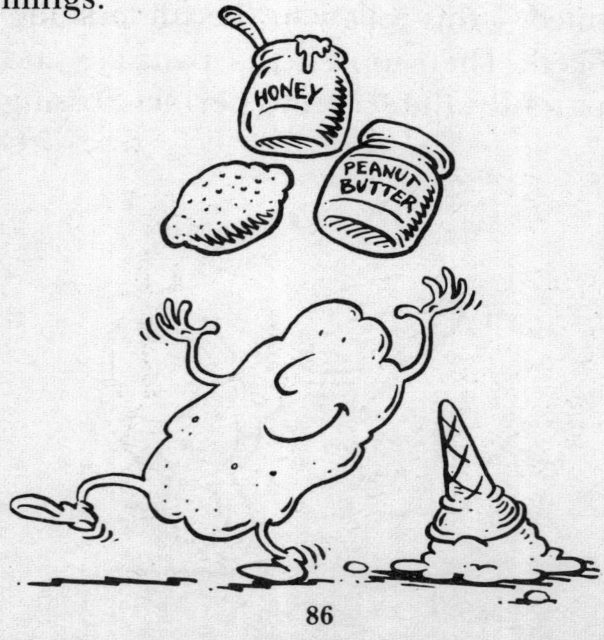

How we did it (i.e. How not to do it!)
Well, we did everything wrong!
1. The butter was not hot enough.
2. We put too much batter in the pan.
3. We tossed the pancake before it was cooked - so most of it ended up on the floor!

A real case of too many cooks spoil the pancakes!

From Jean Boxer,
Silsden, West Yorkshire

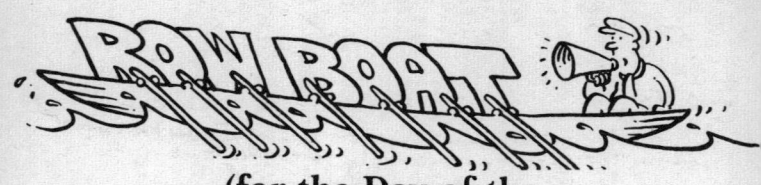

(for the Day of the
Oxford–Cambridge Boat Race)

You need
1 Swiss roll
1 small block of ice-cream
8 tinned or fresh strawberries
8 wooden or plastic ice-cream spoons
Cake decoration/flag

What to do
Cut the Swiss roll into nine pieces, and
the ice-cream into eight slices. Arrange

them alternatively down a long narrow
dish. Put a strawberry on each slice of
ice-cream – these represent the team's

heads. Put four spoons on each side of the boat, sticking them into the ice-cream, to make oars. Put a flag with your

team's colours on one end for a finishing touch. I tried making this with Strawberry Switchblade (very appropriate we thought!), but our boat very definitely sank! We blamed it on bad weather!

From Katie Harding,
Somerset

EASTER CHICKENS

What you need
1 block of marzipan
1 cream egg
Chocolate buttons
Smarties
Cocktail sticks
Currants

What to do
Roll out the marzipan and use most of it to cover the cream egg. Use the rest to

roll into a ball for a head. Use chocolate buttons for eyes, and cut an orange-coloured Smartie in half for the beak.

Break a cocktail stick in half and use the two pieces as legs, putting currants at the bottom for feet. Hope they're not too tweet for you!

From Paul Bourgeouis,
Hailsham, East Sussex

SUMMER HATS

What you need
3 tablespoons icing sugar
1 teaspoon water
1 marshmallow
1 digestive biscuit
Hundreds and thousands/iced flowers/
silver balls

What to do
Mix the icing sugar and the water to
form a paste. 'Stick' the marshmallow on

to the biscuit with the icing paste. Deco-

rate with hundreds and thousands, iced flowers and silver balls.

From Elizabeth Small,
Grimsby

Luscious Liquids

SUNSET COCKTAIL

What to line up
Concentrated orange
Water
Blackcurrant juice
Cherries
Pineapple chunks
Cocktail sticks

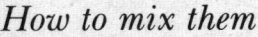

How to mix them
Pour the concentrated orange into the bottom of a tall glass. Fill it with water,

then slowly pour the blackcurrant down the inside of the glass. It should settle nicely at the bottom. *Do not stir!* Put some cherries and pineapple chunks on a cocktail stick and balance in the drink.

From Julian and Christian Redman,
Dover, Kent

WITCHES BLOOD

This is a variation of Sunset Cocktail: if you mix together Coca-Cola, Ribena and orange juice, then the colour becomes a

dark red, like blood. Try pretending to your friends that it's Witches' Blood!

From Catherine Mole,
Basingstoke, Hampshire

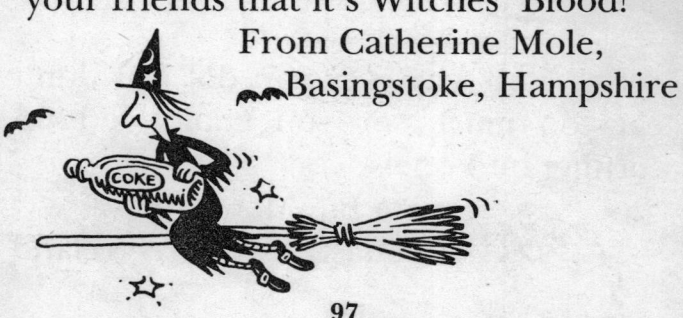

Blob Juice

Blob bits
1 cup yoghurt
1 cup grape juice

How to make the blob
Mix the two ingredients together and you can't go wrong – you end up with a

green blob whatever you do! But don't eat too much, or you could end up turning into one!

From Ian McDowell,
Belfast, Northern Ireland

LEMON FIZZ

What you need
1 lemon
Caster sugar
Ice
Soda water

What to do
Squeeze the juice from the lemon (watch out for cut fingers – it can sting!). Pour it

into a glass and add one teaspoon of caster sugar. Add some crushed ice, and

then fill to the brim with soda water. Add more sugar to taste. We give this to James to wake him up in the morning!

From Carol Lightfoot,
Silloth

Banana Bonanzas

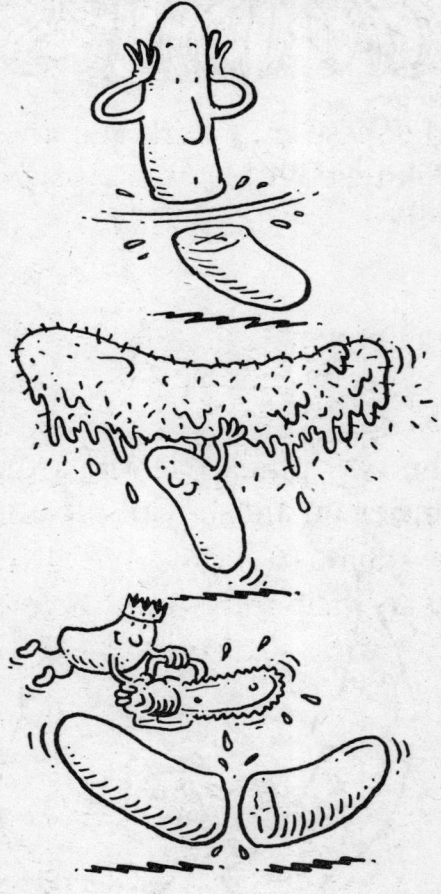

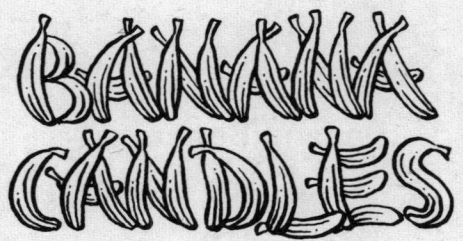

BANANA CANDLES

What you need
2 pineapple rings
1 banana
Jam
Nuts
Glacé cherry

What to do
Put the two pineapple rings on top of each other on a dish. Cut off one end of

the banana so that it stands straight – roll it in jam and nuts and then stand in the middle of the rings. Cut the cherry into a

petal shape, and place it on top for the flame. What you might call a candlelit dinner!

> From Kay Harvey,
> Stockbridge, Hampshire

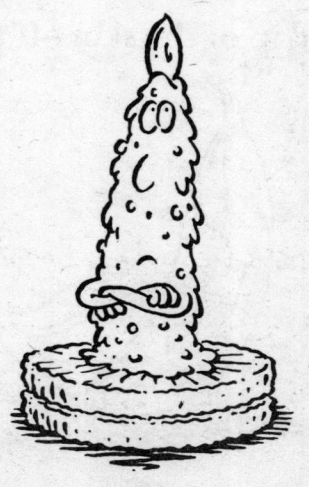

BANANA BABY

What you need
1½ bananas
Honey
Hundreds
and thousands
2 sultanas
½ cherry
Cream

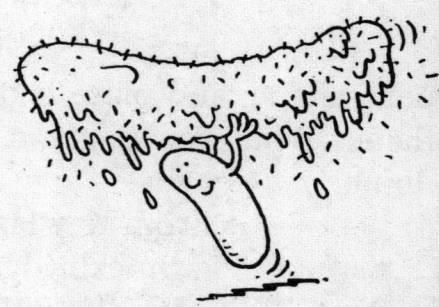

What to do
Peel one strip of the skin off the banana,

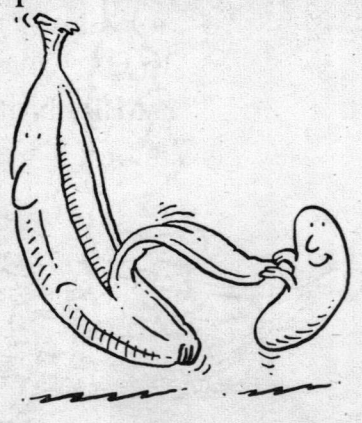

and then remove the fruit inside. Dip the banana in honey, cover in hundreds and thousands and then place it back in the skin. Use the sultanas as eyes, the cherry

as a nose, and then spray the cream round the face for hair. Cut the other half banana to look like arms.

From Kerry Langton,
Milt, Nottinghamshire

BANANA LOLLIPOP

(Royal Bananas)

What you need
1 banana
Golden syrup
Grated chocolate/crushed digestive
biscuits

What to do
We call these royal bananas because I
made them with H.R.H. Prince Edward.
He coped excellently, and so should you!
Cut the banana in half, roll in golden

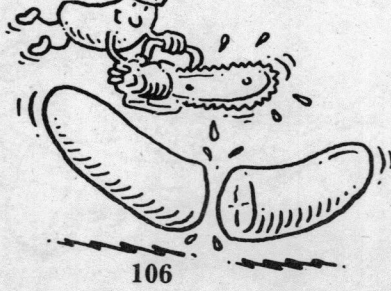

syrup, and then cover in grated chocolate or crushed digestive biscuits. Then

put on the end of a lollipop stick.
From Christopher Williams,
Ammanford, Dyfed

Tasty Travel

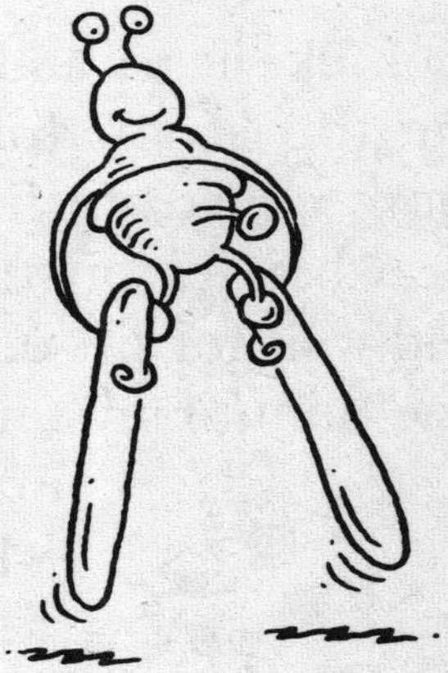

Parts

Ice-cream
Strawberry jam
Chocolate fingers
Chunks of orange
2 strawberries

How to construct

Put two scoops of ice-cream on a plate, one on top of the other. Spread the jam

around the bottom scoop. Place the chocolate fingers around the bottom to

look like legs, and chunks of orange in the top scoop for windows. Stick two more chocolate fingers in the top with strawberries on the end for antennae, and wait for lift-off! To be eaten during one-minute mysteries!

From Nicholas Baker,
Portslade, East Sussex

RACING CAR

What you need
1 large carrot
1 slice of ham
Ketchup
2 slices of bread
6 cocktail sticks

The mechanics
Take out the middle of the carrot for the

driving seat, and cover with the ham and
ketchup. Roll the bread into four balls

(wheels), spike with the cocktail sticks (axles), and then place on either side of the carrot. The trouble is, one lap and it's gone!

From Domenica Politano,
Corby, Northamptonshire

RAFT RACER

What you need
1 French stick
Butter
Tomatoes
Cucumber
Slices of processed
cheese
Cocktail sticks
Lettuce

What to do
Cut the French stick into lengths, and then cut down the middle. Butter each

side and cover with slices of tomato and cucumber. Cut the slices of processed cheese into triangles, thread on to the cocktail sticks, and place in the middle of

the rafts for sails. Place on a bed of lettuce for the water. Keep these for rafters!

From Nicola Horne,
   Cannock, Staffordshire

Mishmash

THE PHANTOM GRAVE

Here lies the grave of
a poor old sinner,
who died of eating
cold school dinners!

Ghoulish ingredients
1 sausage
1 thin finger of bread
Tomato sauce
Grated cheese

What to do
Cut the middle section out of the sau-

sage – this is the grave. Lay the finger of bread inside, and cover with grated

cheese. Sprinkle on tomato ketchup to make it look lifelike. Cut the top off the

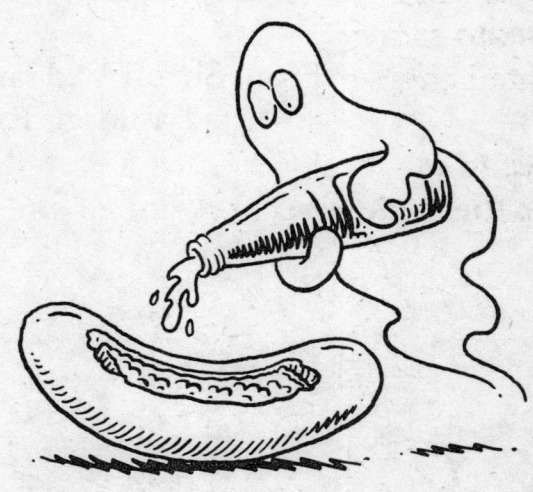

discarded section of the sausage and place at the head of the grave – this is the

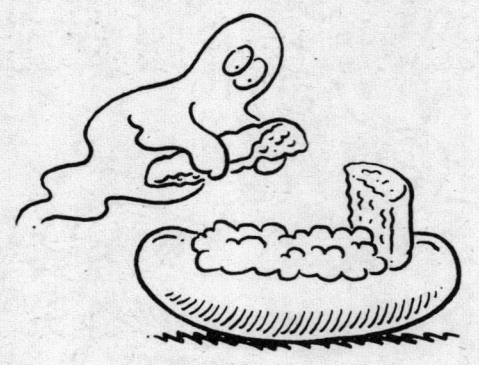

tombstone. Then put back the remaining sausage for the lid of the coffin. A real blood-sucking meal – the best time to eat this is during *Ghosts, Monsters and Legends*.

From Shruti Vadgarna,
Basildon, Essex

BROWNIE MUSHROOMS

What you need
2 eggs
Lettuce leaves
1 tomato

What you do
Boil the eggs until hard. Shell when cold

and cut off the bottoms so they stand on
end. Arrange the lettuce leaves on a dish

and stand the eggs on it. Cut the tomato
in half, remove the inside and place each

half on top of an egg. Cut the excess egg white into bits, and sprinkle on the top of the tomatoes to give your mushrooms spots.

From Michelle Boness,
Bridgend, Wales

A MATCHBOX

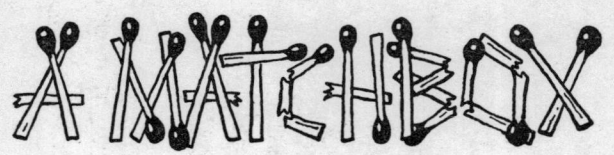

What you need
2 slices of bread
Butter
Chips
Tomato sauce

What to do
Butter the bread and cut a quarter off

the top of one slice. Place a row of chips
upright on the whole piece of bread, and
put a blob of tomato sauce at the end of
each chip. Then lay the other slice of

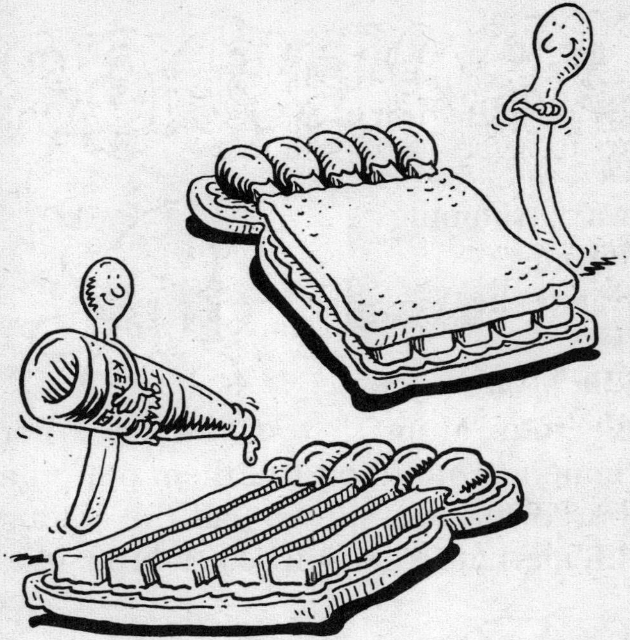

bread back on top. What you might call light at the end of the lunchbox, or chips on strike!

From Cara Blay,
Reading, Berkshire

MARMITE FINGERS

What you need
Pastry trimmings
Marmite
Grated cheese

What to do
Ask your Mum if you can have her trimmings, and then roll them out on a floured surface. Spread half the oblong with marmite, then sprinkle a little grat-

ed cheese on top. Fold the other half over, press the edges down lightly and cut into fingers. Place on a greased tray and bake for 10–15 minutes at 375°F, gas mark 5.

From Louise Bispham,
Bury, Lancashire

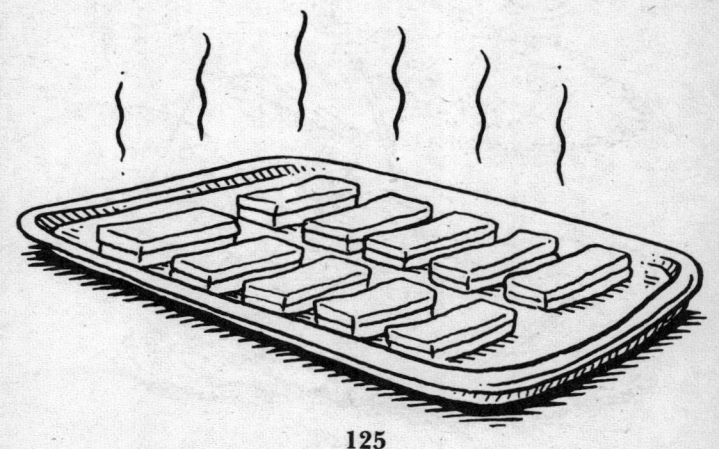

BOOK SNACK

Contents
3 slices of cheese
2 slices of bread
Tomato ketchup

How to bind it
Put a slice of cheese on top of a slice of bread. Get a cocktail stick, dip it in the tomato ketchup and write on the cheese. If you come to a word you know you can't spell, you say bonk, and if you get it wrong it's a boob!

Do the same with the other pieces of cheese – these become the pages of the book. Put the second slice of bread on

top as the cover. Now you know how we got the expression 'eating your words'!

From Stephanie Ward,
Launceston, Cornwall

If you would like to receive a Newsletter about our new Children's books, just fill in the coupon below with your name and address (or copy it onto a separate piece of paper if you don't want to spoil your book) and send it to:

The Children's Books Editor
Young Corgi Books
61–63 Uxbridge Road
Ealing
London W5 5SA

Please send me a Children's Newsletter:

Name: ....

Address: ....

....

....

All the books on the previous pages are available at your local bookshop or can be ordered direct from the publishers: Cash Sales Dept., Transworld Publishers Ltd., 61–63 Uxbridge Road, Ealing, London W5 5SA.

Please enclose the cost of the book(s), together with the following for postage and packing costs:

Orders up to a value of £5.00   50p
Orders of a value over £5.00   Free

Please note that payment should be made by cheque or postal order in £ sterling.